FULL STOPS IN WINTER BRANCHES

Char March grew up in Scotland's run-down industrial belt in the 1960s, and now divides her time between the Yorkshire Pennines and Lochaber. She is a multi-award-winning author, with five poetry collections, six BBC Radio 4 dramas, eight stage plays, two screenplays and a short story collection to her name.

Full Stops in Winter Branches

CHAR MARCH

Valley Press

First published in 2018 by Valley Press
Woodend, The Crescent, Scarborough, YO11 2PW
www.valleypressuk.com

First edition, second printing (November 2018)

ISBN 978-1-912436-11-8
Cat. no. VP0131

Cover and text design by Jamie McGarry.

Printed and bound in Great Britain by
TJ International Ltd, Padstow, Cornwall.

Contents

*for everyone who has
encouraged me to keep going*

An enthusiasm

It got wearing when every menu
had to be corrected before we could eat.

When you began to carry permanent markers
– in six colours – in every handbag.

When I took you for rambles, and signposts,
farm produce boards, interpretation leaflets

all had to be axed of excess apostrophes, split
infinitives, eccentric spelling.

When you'd rant for hours on the phone
to Hong Kong, Poland and Mumbai

over imperfect instructions for your hoover,
flat-pack bedside table, packet of crisps.

Aunt Patricia nearly went through the windscreen
when you threw on the anchors on the M62,

then ran across all four lanes to draw a semi-colon
on that roadworks sign.

You sent corrected letters (furious with red ink)
back to MPs, Yorkshire Water, our children.

You stalked the length of every train, bifocals
cocked at each and every notice.

You made the guard reword his announcements,
and practise – three times – over the tannoy.

You bought sticker sheets of punctuation,
sent the grandchildren off with bunches

of commas, en-dashes, question marks.
You bought pallet-loads of *Eats, Shoots & Leaves*,

handed them out evangelically at the WI, yoga,
outside Sainsbury's, and to every teacher you met.

I got my revenge on your gravestone.

They just use dogs to get more dosh –
it shouldn't be allowed

*(Title as heard on a BBC Radio Leeds phone-in
about people sleeping rough in the city.)*

This is my person
He sleeps beside me

I've had him for two years,
found him in a Waitrose car park

I brought him some newspapers
My person likes newspapers – and cardboard

He gave me a cream cake from the bin
He tied himself to me with this string

This is our home
It glitters with smells

It is best in winter
Then the metal tubes blow hot air

In summer it is cars' barks
And there are loud people

They come and kick my person
They try to kick me

Sometimes he is sick
I eat his sick

Then I take him to the big place that echoes
They give him a hot bowl

They give me crunchy bits and a stroke
Then they scare my person with pieces of paper

He takes his cardboard
He takes my blanket

I lead him back home

Praise-prayer to Leeds from Rattus norvegicus

Dearest Leeds, we thank you for your sewers:
for our subterranean superhighways lead us into temptation

We thank you for the cacophony of scents and stinks
your pavements give us, their lush squishings of Tetley's and chips

We thank you for going fortnightly with your bin collections,
and for your Loiners who liberally spread offerings to us

We thank you for dim street lighting so we may guzzle in peace;
we thank you for The Dark Arches where we hold our AGMs

We thank you for providing loft insulation and wiring to gnaw
from Adel to Armley, Beeston to Calverley, Horsforth to Seacroft

We thank you for all the cosy homes you provide for us,
for all your roof spaces and cavity walls, for every under-floor

We thank you for constant food and warmth; for every landfill,
especially the thrice-odiferous Micklefield site

We thank you for making your Environment Officers focus on
our flying brethren, rather than us, with their nets and poisons

We thank you for inviting us unto your great cityness
with your welcome flag of a dead sheep

And we sing together *Muroidea Muroidea Muroidea Amen*

The inter-species dialogue of Columba palumbus

We commune with children in Roundhay Park;
and old men with time in their pockets:

their sudden runs and jerked laughter;
their overcoats and paper-bag crumbs

are messages heavy with Loiner philosophy
and we join the debate with our tonal coo-cooing,

our head-bobbing, the exact way we strut.

We circumnavigate your air, write white
hieroglyphs on the columns of Temple Works,

eat the crinkle-cut chips you proffer
in a precise order that speaks volumes

of our multiverse roosts, of the iridescent
galaxies to which we fly when Millennium Square

kicks out your last drunk, and the Civic Hall's
golden clock tocks past three.

Kestrel versus crow

I am fence-post turned to glide
I follow black line across
hard white ground

my eyes are flicker
tree-light-tree-light-tree-light

I am soar

white ground is hedge-squared
the line where ground and air roost
is pylon-pinned is tilt-tilt-level-tilt-level-tilt

my eyes snag black-flap

I am hunt

black-flap is below
black-flap is caw-caw
black-flap is slow flap

I am pursuit

I am hedge tree sky
I steer in scream-wind
tilt-tilt-level-tilt-level-tilt

I am tension

I am dive-strain
I am scream-wind
I am talons

black-flap is caw-caw
he is flurry-swerve
twig-crash

I am thump, snatch, roll, neck-nip

black-flap is ground
my beak, blood

Ardnamurchan dragonfly

To capture the colour of energy
intact, we tie the bag mouth

over the hot chug-fug
of the car's exhaust.

We'd watched it flit
all morning over the lochan;

mate tail-to-tail in mid-air;
hover over opening water-lilies.

We coveted its shimmering,
that pencil-torch of ultramarine.

Now, caught in the blown globe
of a clear plastic bag

it is frantic moth-in-a-lampshade fizz,
wings an iridescent buzz.

We sweat for minutes,
the clattering blur

not winding down.

The two of us squatting
coughing shifting.

Finally the slim brilliance
stops.

And its colour clicks off
– death a lightswitch.

Dad shuts off the engine,
avoids my eyes.

I bury the beige twig.

Nest

to snuggle to coorie doon to snoodle.
a half-world of care.

a gowpen of shoogling eggs
roofed by warm breast.

a weaving of twigs.
eaves studded with river-mud huts.

a precariousness in wind.
a responsibility of worms, sand eels, gnats.

a rock ledge with fifty thousand screams.
the heart of a hedge.

full stops in winter branches
each a basket of hope.

Bee-dance

This is the anther, this the stamen
This the petal, this the carpel
This is the slap, this the tickle
This is the caress of downy body
This is her furred leg
laden with golden bulge
– a pulse of brightness –
that shows she's been raiding
nectaries since dawn.

Tipsy with her sugary suckings
she staggers her pollened limbs
through air thick with dusk,
back to her alchemical sisters
who transmute flower-hoard
into glistening energy; eager drones;
and, in the brood chamber
at the colony's heart,
the odd queen.

I am waltzing to you, my busy lovelies,
coming to burgle back my garden's gold,
break into your every cell, swarm
all over you whispering smoky
kisses, all honey-tongued.
Clutching substitute bags
of Tate and Lyle, as if that
will make you
sweet on me.

Salmo salar

She hangs in the autumn water,
a kite in her element
tugged by river-wind.

Her nose searches the currents
for scents of the gravel bed
where she became.

That spring remembered
when she pushed from her redd,
between boulders big as her alevin self.

Through the massacre
of frogs, trout, herons
she has transformed:

fry, then parr,
then her smolt-self sucks salt,
slips from her natal stream;

grows as an ocean grilse, wary
of skate, cod, seals, sharks until,
belly fat with three thousand lives,

she snouts out this stream,
fans and writhes in a cloud of milt
over this river gravel.

Now kelt, exhausted,
she turns through the bodies
of dying cock fish,

her hunger pulling her
back to the salt,
the salt.

So many trees are drowning themselves in you

You are dark opaque
your pelt slicks locks,
numbs hands, slobbers dogs.

You are Ophelia's narrow bed,
the cradler of boats' dreams,
nursery of sticklebacks,

stocked with pike-teeth, traffic cones,
and knives that shouldn't
have gone in that deep.

In rain you show no-one.
In wind you are flutterings of light.
Only in calm sun do you allow

an inversion of boats, ducks,
ash trees, cyclists, a swan, me
– all deep in your alternate universe.

Coppice

He moves among us tenderly
with chainsaw and big hands.
A slight tipping of his head
as we fall to his touch.

We saw off his father
last year – a clutching
at his heartwood as he went down,
then cradled him in our fallen hands
till morning brought the son.

He stacks our grey limbs neat
beside the gouge of track
his father's father laid down,
wipes our rough skinflakes
down his mesh-mailed legs.

Already we are growing back:
a thousand gorgons
pushing tongues of ourselves
through soil to give voice
under his son's saw.

Necessary equipment for River Pigs

A plaid mackinaw, quilt-lined
with layers of saved rags sewn
rough to pocket air; a double-wall
hat – old horse blanket is good;

only dumbfools don't wear no
gloves – rawhide and thick as jerky,
or your hands'll wear clean to bone
in a day hauling peaveys and pike poles;

boots you can trust.

You hammer three nails –
wrought, not cast, your life
hangs on those spikes – one here,
slanty forward from your boot-toe;

two here and here through the heel.
Plug tobacco to keep your breath
real fresh for all the ladies you'll
never see; enough liquor to get you

snokked every night

so's you can sleep
in the dug-down cold here.
The best birling boys are the Irish
– feet quick from the dancing,

and a rare luck on them.
This limp? One leg three-inch
short – logs part, then snap shut
worse nor any beaver trap.

The straight lines of sea areas

This is the shape of the sea in Malin:
northerly backing westerly; good.
Herring catches down, Mallaig ailing
cod endangered, glass falling.

This is the taste of the sea in Hebrides:
herring-gulls – eggs a salt-fish-ness,
guga on their second boiling,
crofts hooded with rain; occasionally poor.

This is the feel of the sea in Rockall:
kelp slippyness, moon shards rough
or very rough, wracks of stormcloud,
heavy swell all the way to Maine.

This is the sound of the sea in Bailey:
a shrieking of white horses,
teeth veering Force Eight; severe.
While, on sea bottom, boulders grind.

This is the smell of the sea in Faeroes:
guano, boat diesel and Famous Grouse,
a tang of icebergs calving away North,
the lonely scent of coconuts on the Jetstream.

Charm for croup

Whelks is an ugly word
when they are a collective noun
of chinking that nestle her neck;
tiny roosting birds
in a camouflage of greys
on a red string of hope.

> Her breathing is stridor, fractured.
> Her clavicles fragile as wishbones

Here is the cold compress,
here the father's slow caress
of forehead, forearms, fingers
while the mother gowpens feet
that have not yet walked, her mouth
moving round old words.

> barely rising, barely falling
> while the whelk-shells chingle

The awl lies on the night-stand.
His palm is raw. Four days now, of
twin holes in each thick-lipped home.
Outside, the rain tries to wash
the smashed three days
from the back of the axe.

> a scuttling of brief chimes
> between each dog-bark-cough.

Where the sea sucks at limpets,
fresh whelks are walking
their one-legged way into
the next day's charm, and,
perhaps, a sea-salt sound
of slightly deeper breaths.

Horses always look cleverer than they are

He doesn't trust their aristocratic eyelashes.
He skirts wide of their paddock
on his plod to the scaffolded church;
never fills his slake bucket from their tap.

The hacking-out takes longer than he'd hoped, his palms
blistered from the plugging-chisel's punishment.
Every afternoon they pound the bounds of their field
as he pounds the mortar joints, clears the Victorian cement.

He's memorised every medieval mason's mark on this East wall
– the weather wall where the sandstone's been ploughed
and globbed by centuries of wind from the Urals.
And every afternoon they kick up their hooves and whinny.

Through August he mixes the quicklime, the sand
– watches each patted-down volcano rise and steam.
Sometimes, when the sizzling slows, he eases his back
against the hot mound. Then hears them nicker and blow.

By October, he's pleased with the re-pointing,
his mortar glows white as the evenings draw in.
He cleaves the clod-awkward chert, knaps the faces blank.
They snort and windsuck as the first frosts breathe at his back.

November. His finger-ends split from flint and the wind
that chews this place, he prinks the nave wall flushwork.
It is the last afternoon that, up through his ladder's feet,
he will feel them beat their strange symbols into the turf.

Over and over where her neck made that final sound.

Jam

You can store summer in jamjars:
the sun the smell the colour of long days
and then, in the crapness of January,
open the cupboard and see

all those jars of jam that made the place
drip with steam, that never set, that are already
choked with mould and tell you nothing
about seasons, but loads about how you've

never been a proper woman because a proper woman
would be able to bake a decent cake, write
a shopping list and stick to it, make a child
laugh, remember to wipe the washing line

before pegging out all his white shirts, apply
mascara in the rearview without sobbing, eke
out the housekeeping, peel an apple without
breaking the skin, pick all the lentils

from the fire's ashes,
weave nettles into swans.

She stirs the slurring strawberries
that look like cervical cysts. She's already
thrown up in the sink twice this morning,
has missed her hair appointment

Can't you get yourself looking nice for once?
has forgotten to take her pills, has spotted
moths in the jumper drawer and that everything
is unravelling at a faster rate

than usual this week.

What's in the tin?

It's a guinea pig asleep.
A cake spiked by skewers,
fed on brandy for months.

Izal toilet paper and those
lady-in-a-crinoline paper bags.
It's all the pens I've ever lost.
My third miscarriage.

That robin that flew into
the kitchen window and left
a perfect dust-print of itself

and we tried to revive with drips
of sugared water from
your ear-syringe.

It's cockle-shaped pralines
each set in its own
green velvet bed.

That willow-pattern side plate
you smashed over my head
last week when I told you

about the affair, and that you
stuck back together
with rose petals.

If I shook the tin – gently –

I'd hear claws scrabbling,
the thud of furry body off-
balance, perhaps that strange
fluting plea for dandelions.

My third miscarriage would
be a desiccated slide
as caul and non-life whisper
across rusty tin-plate.

The kettle has boiled.
She approaches the table
– where I now seem to live.
She holds the teapot like a gun.
She opens the tin.

Sarah Ann Henley work-shadows the Suicide Tsar

We know there is a continuum
of risk factors – a gradually rising slope,
ending in a bridge… a precipice.

Along its windy edge we join hands:
a paperchain of figures, of research papers,
of probabilities, of delaying tactics.

We try to create in you the gravitational pull
of carrots: of being wanted; of wanting to be;
to stay with us – the living.

And we are shameless – we'll use
sticks too: that insistent tug of duty,
your fear of pain, your terror

of it not working – of you being left
vegetable. We'll brandish the hurt
you'll sear – forever – into others.

If nothing else works (though it goes
against our grain) we'll even call in religion
if it will help… Help keep you here:

till the Never Event stays… never;
till your weather clears;
till the breeze re-sets your sails.

Keeping them all in the air

Juggling balls are not guinea pigs,
brandied cake, sanitary shame,
disappeared biros, possible baby,
dead robin, bedded chocolates,
a badly-repaired marriage.

They are the palm-slap
of others' hand-grease; cool
and fat, and hiding
their stitches.

They are primary-coloured
concentration; a need
to stand; to have
room; to reach
into air.

The usefulness of weather

She is looking at me in that
here-is-a-social-pause way. I say
There was 66% cloud cover yesterday.
In the waiting room, I had checked
the Met Office site,
so I could be accurate, not general.

But I know general comments
are also applicable.
Later I will say
It's been a mild winter.
But I know, now, not to add
the figures that back this statement:
the mean average since records began;
the three exceptional years
of which this is one;
the fact that, of the 10 mildest winters,
8 have occurred in the last 15 years.

I see she has given me
another social pause
or perhaps she has asked a question.
I study her for clues:
the pen tapping; the forms
still on page 1; the sigh.

I tell her my name.
Then, rather rashly add
It's a good day for washing
though, as I say this,
my glance to the window shows
it is now raining
in a North Easterly direction
with a wind speed
of approximately 25mph.

Nostalgia for hot aches

We built an igloo every November on the back lawn
and lived in it till the April melt.

We rolled snowmen bigger than planets that stood sentinel
on the rockery – our Falkirk moai.

All mud was permafrost, all lochs solid, all waterfalls
ribbed ice organ-pipes.

We tobogganed every day, and every day was bright blue
and clear moon, every window was fern-frost

that the coal fire couldn't melt till noon in pools on every sill.
We took off our jumpers maybe twice a year.

Global Warming sounded lovely till the reality:
mud-slop paths, rain and rain and more rain,

floods and landslips, grey-on-grey months, an end
to seasons, a never-seen sun.

The sixth roll of the dice

Into the small square lawn
five diamonds are cut that stun
everyone with colour,
every summer.

These roses never get blackspot,
or the thousand other cankers
that silence flesh. Just
flourish. Velvet and thorned.

They are my brothers, my
sisters – cauled and curled.
Before the drug that glued me
full-term. Scrambled

my inumme stysem.

We are The Psoriasis Warriors

We are capable of making our skins erupt
volcanoes of plaques that spout pain,
our scalps are fabulous helmets of itch,
our testicles great balls of fire!

You live in a cold world of perfection
your hands smooth, your legs polished,
when you swim no-one runs shrieking
from the pool, you turn no heads.

We buzz with steroids, slather ourselves
with the stench of coal tar, we are guttate,
pustular, flexular – they try to stun us
to normality with their UV rayguns.

You complain of slightly the wrong
shade of honey blonde tan,
while you cram us into burqas
to not offend your world's sight.

But we burst out, scarlet skin-armour
gleaming, splitting with pride,
raging with the heat of battling
this world that loves bland.

The finding of parts

I thought my granddad
a sailor of The High Seas, for,
in my picturebooks,
only pirates had tattoos,

and scars. He played along
with my stories of the ink
blurs on his arms, *Arr, Jim Lad.*
Doubloons and a purple parrot!

Thirty years later, I found
the dusty box of tapes; got
the reel-to-reel machine
working again. Heard

my dead father's *One-Two, One-Two.*
Then granddad's gravel
spooling out: the quivering
candle in the dug-out;

the Quink Permanent in a tin mug;
the needle passed round;
the extra ration of rum;
the wincing of each lad.

All that week his platoon
had been on Collecting Duty out
in No-Man's – picking up
bits of their dead mates,

and failing to match them up.

So each unique design was scraped
into him by one of his KOYLI mates;
into each forearm, each bicep,
each calf, then torso, back, neck.

They'd each sat, bleeding, proud
they'd faced the pain; puffing
on Navy Cut. And then,
tongues pressed between teeth,

drew on the fly-leaf of their
1915 Soldier's Diary, each tat.
Here is the stick-figure he drew
– transfixed with arrows –

my granddad as St Sebastian.
At each arrow's flight-feathers
a cramped sketch that meant:
Private John Henry Taylor's

left forearm, right calf, …

It was summat we could do
granddad crackles from the tape
sucking on his pipe, sucking again.
So we could be… A rattling cough.

So all of us could be safely gathered in.
And then there is his dry laugh,
and the tape – softly clattering
its red tail round, and round.

Lest we forget?

This quiet graveyard is now eulogised
as 'wildflower-friendly': Eggs-And-Bacon
thread through Ladies' Bedstraw and Self-Heal.

The Norman porch displays a list
of the one hundred and three lichen species
found by the enthusiastic British Lichen Society

including the rare *Myriospora smaragdula*.

We stroll through knee-high Yorkshire Fog
and Sweet Vernal Grass mouthing
the graves' names, their ages.

Turn a verdant corner and
come upon them: scoured,
buzz-cut, rawly new.

Do they want this regimented scrubbing?

This forever standing to attention:
All-ready-for-inspection-sir!
Why not let this 19 year old, this 22 year old,

this Private, this Lieutenant develop a skin
of lichen, a suit of moss, a softening
of bird-splatter?

Do they want their grasses and wildflowers
shaved to within a millimetre of their soil?
Does this six-monthly assault with electric sander

comfort them?

Or do they wish to rest, to lie
hammocked in the curve of the earth,
to become one with the bearded graves

that cluster round them, that lean in
like ears, like hands ready to soothe,
while the soldiers stand to attention

in uniforms stiff with bleach.

The unreality of surfaces

It is said by those who know
that there are lightyears of space
between a nucleus and its electrons.

That electrons orbit in unknowable
ways as far from their home planet
as the Oort Cloud is from Mercury – further

in fact. For those-who-know relish facts.
And it is a fact that we are made up.
Made up almost entirely of space.

Forget being made almost entirely of water.
That is a different fact, by others
who think on a different scale.

Forget that other-people-who-know
now tell us that we are composed primarily
of things not even human.

Forget that second genome, just
concentrate on those vast tracts
in our – and our microbes' – every atom.

There is so much space
so much nothingness
within each atom of me

it is a recurring miracle I can feel
anything. This table top, this teacup, her eye
studying my mouth.

And so, through nothingness
we travel. Elliptically orbit one another.
Until there are fewer, and fewer,

and fewer molecules of nitrogen,
of oxygen, of those trace atmospheric
gases holding us apart. Then

the unbelievability of these particles
– the outer outer edges of my lips –
jostling a strange electron dance

against the whirl
of unseeable charges
that are her nape.

This is the talking of hands

My talk. Not yours.
Your hands are clumsy, inaccurate,
fumble things round the twisted way.
Your eyes tell me they hold my pain,
but you know nothing of pain,
or the holding of it, or the way
pain held me in joy. You know nothing
of joy. You want to know only of pain,
as if this is the significant thing.

My daughter is eight years old, and makes
the stage look very big. I strapped her feet
into the gold sandals. She is dipping,
her back a swan's neck, her fingers
arch back in perfect half-moons.
She smiles. Her seed-pearl teeth gleam. She smiles.
She quivers the long golden nails that I tied
with wire into her fingertips.

These are the exercises to get the hands to bend.
This is the stinging oil that is massaged in hot,
this is the leather-lined vice, this is the repetition,
this is the repetition, this is the repetition.
It must all begin at suckling age.
The exercises, the oil, the vice.

This is the talking of hands. My voice
is clear and sharp. High as a laughingthrush call.
Yours, the muffled crashing of rhino
in forest far off. Your fingers are stubby,
and banded with white from your vanished rings.
We have all seen how your eyes slide on our sons.

Your hands mumble, mutter, stutter, stumble.
They can never catch the quickness of our speech,
the deftness of my laughter at you. They are never
going to wring the neck of a junglefowl, they speak
with slithering marks on paper, they are hands
to smother life from something,
not give it a clean end.

This is where my hands used to be

Vapourised de-fusing the booby trap. Took
a goat with them. I kept the other guys safe
though. Maybe there's a goat *Jannah*
with extra good grass, eh?

The CO found my left thumb. Stuck to the APC's
windscreen. Looks just like my Dad's. The Doc
gave me the formaldehyde. Said this Damien guy
made millions from dead stuff – floating.

Quite a few ops. But I've got great stumps.
Never get chafing from these new pincers. They
can grip an axe now. Before, I had to use dynamite
to turn my trees to kindling.

Last time I was down in Glasgow, they said touch
might be an option. Damn near cried. That's how come
me and the wife split. Couldn't feel her. But
touch, eh? That's well worth fighting for.

The F word

I am flow and flux; I am contradiction
I protect teeth, and corrode glass
I am incendiary bombs, and Prozac
I make metal melt, and fridges cold

Only 12 elements on Earth are > me
I ∧ global warming and ∨ your cholesterol
I killed chemists who tried to isolate me
Plants use me to ward off wildebeest

I am global contaminant,
and ground-breaking artificial blood
I am persistent organic pollutant
and life-saving liquid breathing

I cause G-20 Summits to argue interminably
My homolytic cleavage guzzles ozone
I can warm our planet
20,000 × faster than CO_2

I am nuclear fission, and Teflon
I am surfactant, and anaesthetic
I am catalyst, and date-rape drug
I am asthma puffer, and can make water burn

I am pale and yellow and gas and lethal,
and Derbyshire Blue John grockle trap
I am phobic about water, and loathe fat
I am utterly irresistible to electrons

I save premature babies,
and am deadlier than cyanide
I am Moissan's 'savage beast'
and you have yet to tame me.

High Fidelity

It is the end of the shift when my hair falls loose:
a single strand of me catches in the sticky tape;
that pin-prick-tug on scalp as I lean forward
to nestle speakers into polystyrene.

> I used to wonder what music, what
> voices, would make those dark bowls
> flex behind their stretched brown cloth.
> What type of silences they'd cup.

Already the open box is juddering away
down the black tongue of belt,
smuggling that thread of me away.
My hands hang, heavy as sacks of rice.

> I imagined music like large-drop rain;
> like feet gliding through paddy field mud;
> speech like butterflies in the high bamboo;
> news sturdy as headlights.

Zhang Bao slaps on her A1 label;
the metal arms slam the box
shut; the roller parcel-tapes it tight;
and a whisper of me is stowaway.

> What remains of me here just hears the dirge
> of the rent, the moaning chant of when the train fare
> can be scrimped – to return to Qiang who is now three
> and has no memory of my voice.

Connection

He is the music buff, I am simply eager
for the polystyrene – perfect drainage
in our biggest plant pots – so snatch
at the nestled speakers. He is steadier;

unpacks the hi-fi ponderously, ticks off
each item on the *How To Assemble* leaflet.
It is because he slows me down
that I find her. Caught in the sellotape.

We are both bent and white now, but she
is jet black, lustrous, long. I hold her
to the morning light spreading through
the mimosa. Is she in Korea or Taiwan,

Hanoi or Beijing; sweat-shop or gleaming factory?
Held to my centre parting, her length drops
to my nipple. Did her nape knot come undone?
Did she feel the tug as the sellotape trapped her,

carried her to another continent?

I hold her limp across both my palms,
show her to him. We both look East.

The monitoring of punches

In the popcorn dark she coldly notes
where each blow lands, and whether,
in the next scene, the cut, the bruise,
the trickle of blood is on the correct side
– or the Continuity Girl needs sacking.

Watching his favourite DVD with her Dad,
she points out the flick-flack of Shane's bruise,
left cheekbone to right, then back. She ruins
Bullitt and *When The Legends Die* for him too
her finger buzzing in the static of the telly screen

as bruises, limps, bloodstains switch sides, switch again.

Her father stops sharing his classics with her.
She re-watches the Terminator movies – on loop;
Arnie continually smashed back to his metal armature.
But she wants a film that shows the actual damage
when a single punch is landed – when a planet of fist hits

the lips of a 16-year-old girl, and those things
that were kissable explode to fringes of pulped
blood, and the lilt of nose doesn't just break, it
concertinas in a splintered mush so nostrils face
front and she is *Pig* for the rest of that corridored year.

Herd

this morning, when he's eating cornflakes,
and yawning, and chatting with his Mum,
and messaging his girlfriend, and streaming music
in the shower, and snapchatting his pals,
and playing Nioh, and fitting in half an hour
of Splatoon with his kid sister, and then racing
Biscuit across the park, and tossing the steaming
black bag into bushes, and throwing the slobbered ball
till his shoulder aches, he's an individual
with a name: Josh

this afternoon, when he pulls on the striped top,
the scarf, buys a packet of Dequadin to get him
through the shouting, and a six-pack to sup
on the bus there, he becomes one of the 21,000
who are sucked from all directions to the plug-hole
of a stadium where they are sluice-gated
into different colours kept distinctly
apart, and he is now an unheard
bellow roaring up the throat of
the 15,452 that are his colour.

Mid-Atlantic ridge

I started moving
around the time
of The Great Oxidation Event;
round about two
and a half
billion years ago.
Yes. A while ago, and
I've not moved far. Well,
not moved at all actually.
Always been just here.
Very slowly shoving
all the Americas West;
everything else East.
At about the same rate
that your little human
fingernails grow.
Nothing, really.
Quite a bit of Atlantic Ocean
now? Yes, I suppose.
But that hectic Ring Of Fire lot,
over in the Pacific. Do you know,
they sometimes move
a couple of metres a year.
Madness.

'Walrus bone carving circa 1810'

Sawn from a rib, this Inuk Eve,
the size of a thumb-joint, peeps
from the dark oval of marrow.

Her scratched face: two slits
for eyes; the mouth a short
held line of smile.

Her shoulders slope
from the scored fur hood
of her sukilpaq parka.

Her neck was brought to life
with short jerks of a blade while
Beau Brummell dandified in Bath.

She fits in the cave of your palm
holding her laughter
like a fresh-caught fish.

Find

Late autumn, and metal blades
have sliced this clay field
into lipped wounds stumbled
with stone clods.

The wind is Siberian, scything
our ankles, skinning our ears
tucked deep into parkas,
muffled by duffel-coats.

We are a straggled line
of bent backs, eyes
down – as eager as bingo –
at these fresh cuts.

My great-grandmother
gleaned these same fields,
pushed out my grandma there –
under a hedge long ripped up.

Cut and knotted the cord
with her clay-clagged hands,
bundled Alice – number eleven –
in her shawl then plodded

the rows again, a Rembrandt
of *Stooping Woman In Potato Field*.
I have the luxury of gleaning
for baubles: agates, carnelian,

the blurred green of serpentine.
Our lapidary club will hum
with pebble-tumblers, and talk
of silver settings, far through winter.

I am sharp-eyed, half the height
of the others – eight years old – while
they rest on sticks, walk
with limps and coughs.

So it's my eyes that fasten
on the gleam of flint, napped
to a deadly delicacy –
an arrow no cupid should fire.

Desk-light

I sow crescent moons
from his laid-aside glasses,
him snoring in the wing-chair
while I read his letter
open on the blotter.

I am sun, hatted with red cloud.
I play with the ceiling,
cobwebs, cracked cornices;
give sideways glances
to the curtains,

open, and letting night
look in. While, suspended
in the dark garden,
my pale twin
flickers with rain.

The flicks

the sprocket-chatter, the racy
flammability of nitrocellulose

the lushness of black and white
the lighting perfect on every cheek

the kindness of Vaseline on the lens
for ageing stars

the smoke spiralling up through
the projector's beam

the crick in your neck
in the front row

the hand up your skirt
in the back row

the trying to open a packet
of Barley Sugar quietly

the rising joy behind your ribs
at the Pearl & Dean music

the smell of much-sat-on velvet
and wet macs

the disappointment that
film stars

(I once bumped into James Mason
in a Kwik-Fit)

are the same size
as you and me

Love potion flask

All day chalking out patterns;
tacking lapels and kick pleats.

Every evening cranking up through
the gears – a Tag-Relay on the track,

or a Time-Trial into that East wind.
And on a weekend it's an Endurance:

organising the girlfriend
to make up enough sarnies;

to be at the right Feeding Station
at the right time; to mix plenty of sugar

in every water bottle; to hold them just so,
her arm straight; not to flinch

as he trams past gasping, stuffing
sarnie into mouth, spare into back pocket,

bottle into cage. The hours flickering
past in hedgerows. The lanolin – slapped

inside his shorts at dawn – leaking
into the weary saddle till, eleven hours in,

207 miles under his belt, a personal best beckoning
in the final blur of light over Little Fransham,

a slick bend brings him down – loose gravel thick
inside a knee, one elbow a knob of snapped bone,

and her a panicked flag of seersucker
running out of the gloom with a tartan thermos.

The Morag Cowe Literary Heritage Trail of Falkirk

This is the site of the bus station where Cowe
spent many hours waiting for a Bluebird bus,
and where she was regularly threatened
by drunks, and boys with cut-throat razors,
references to which appear in her brilliant
twelfth collection: 'I Wanted To Wet Myself'.

This is the street where Cowe's mother
came to buy apple pie from Fishers The Bakers
which she then passed off as pear pie because
Cowe didn't like cooked apple in her teenage years
as revealed in her brilliant poem-series
'My Mother Lied To Me Every Week'

(which definitely secured for her the post of Poet Laureate
after the sudden death – due to an apple pie – of Carol Ann Duffy).

On this site stood the Fine Fare supermarket
– now replaced with a PayDayLoan emporium –
where Cowe's mother did her weekly shop and Cowe
clearly hated their own brand packaging, I quote
from her TS Eliot Prize-winning collection:
the yellow, the awful yellow, the awful yellow.

This blue plaque marks the spot where Cowe
started her first period while out on the hockey field
with only pants and a blouse on because she'd thought
it was swimming that week. A poem in Cowe's juvenilia
references this event but I am unable to quote from it,
Cowe being notoriously cagey about her early works

(before her breakthrough collection
'I've Left All That Behind Me So Shut The Fuck Up').

Sadly the mobile classrooms have long gone where Cowe
began her love of chemistry which features so strongly
in her magnificent 'Periodic Table And Chairs'.
In fact the whole of Cowe's secondary school has
long since been torched – an event celebrated by Cowe
in her one brief return to our town for BBC4's docudrama.

This is the town hall tower from which Cowe
was regularly spat on by other pupils. This resulted
in her mother cutting off most of Cowe's hair
when she was eight because of – and I quote
from Cowe's 'Reasons Never To Return To Falkirk':
'the impossibility of the three gobstoppers /

the five slobs of pink gum / the Regal spittle'
Hair, and lack thereof, is, of course, Cowe's magnificent
leitmotif, with cardinal works such as 'Herbal Essences Suck'.
We now come to the most exciting part of our tour:
the former location of Goldberg's department store
where Cowe encountered her first working escalator…

Brack hexie

It's grund-ebb, an' aw they eyster-catchers
ur stalkin' yon clabber, daubin'
wi' thur lang orange nebs.

Bairns fae Luffness
ur ruggin' whelks fae the rocks,
stechin' thur wee chowks wi' green slake.

They dinna gley – fur ma ill-ee micht claucht theym!
Naetheless, a wean coggles o'er tae gaup, stairts greetin',
aw bubbly-nebbit, aboot ma puir wee pousie.

For she's nailed here wi' me,
tae this muckle stab aside slack-watter merk,
ma shorn hair, her fud, brent oan yon bleize at ma feet.

Mind, yon flams ur no sae nearhaund as tae gie me
a swith awa. Yon wud spyle thur daffin.
Na – slack watter maun turn tae a six-'oor creep.

Brack will tak ma feet, knaps, hurdies,
ma wame, breest, shouder,
ma craig, ma lips wit spat

an' cursed yon man wit
stuck hissel inside o' me,
inside o' me, inside o' me.

If theym guid men huv juidged it richt
it'll stap juist ower ma neb, ablo ma een –
so's I can see theym still

aw lauchin'.

The 'conservation nightmare' of the Ballachulish Goddess

Wit the fuck huv they dun tae ma heid?
I leuk like yon Norwegian wifie wailin oan a pier!
I uised tae be bonnie, wi' a bit o' brawn oan ma banes.
Noo I'm jist a rickle o' banes… aw wizzent!

See yon label – haiverin' oan aboot me haudin'
some 'phallic symbol' in ma haund?
Wit havers! Can theym high-heid-yins no' see
it's a spurtle fur ma parritch?

Gif I'd been yon bowsie bugger Odin, or yon
auld bastart Thor (he hud a mooth oan him that wan)
they'd huv ta'en guid care o' me fur sure!
Wudnae huv let *thair* tadgers dry oot!

Aw ma bits ur yeukie an' raw – ah'v been needin'
a guid claw, a guid drouk, a guid shaggin'
fur centuries! Yous look a poustie laddie, ken.
Aye yoo! Dinnae look awa' – I've got ma wee

quartz e'en fixit oan yur braw bahookie
and ma big scrabbilit fingurs'll be gi'in yoo
an affi guid feel – soon as I bluiter oot this gless.
Whoar ur yous gaun?! I'm needin' ma hochmagandy!

Pogrom – Clifford's Tower, York

Thon driftin' 'aze of roast pork, I tell thee,
it meks me paunch talk. A single 'ot pie since daybreak,
an' nowt since – through all thon 'ectic trammellin'
up an' down't cobbled ginnels. I allus knowed
as 'ow them weren't true men – snufflin' like sows.
But their women! Gods didn't they screech an' 'owl!

See? One of them even bit us! An' run! I'd allus 'eard
they was that fat as 'ow them could 'ardly waddle.
An' then this gurt long wait after all't fun. Wi' me belly
growlin' an' carryin' on. An' bloody crowd swellin' like a boil.
All't sweat done by us few. I just want a bit of summat
for me trouble – for doin' me civic duty.

But there were nowt there. Paintin's, posh tapestries,
but bugger all tha'd want. We'd 'eard their cellars
was groanin' wi' gold, secret siller, an' rubies big
as noses. Likely! Nivver even a kindly cask of ale.
They must 'ave tekken it wi' 'em, an' The Good Lord knows
as 'ow tha can't do that – specially not them lot.

I loved t'tower all lit an' belchin'.
A 'uge chimbley – all leapin' flame. All a-spit
an' a-crackle wi' their fat bones.
Uuuuuurp! Oh – pardon me. It's me belly.
Nivver right wi' nowt in it. An' all on us below,
a sea of Oooooooos! an' Ahhhhhhs! Flickerin' 'ot faces.

All grinnin' up at t'shafts of sparks an' thon grand smell.
By, I could murder a pie. Tha'd think as 'ow
some bugger'd 'ave nous to come round all on us
wi' some pies, some grog, summat – city of bloody merchants!
For none on us'll move, not till it's cooled enough
to get near wi' rakes an' sieves an' bare bloody 'ands!

Sift thro' their ashes, ferret out all't fused coin, all't
gobs of gold an' globs of bracelets what they've thieved off us.
Money-grubbin' 'eathen. Ouf! We're off!
By, it's a gradely press – canst smell our goodly sweat?
'Ere! Thon bastard tower is still 'urling red-'ot
boulders down on us – whose bloody side is it on?

Immigrants abuse Scottish adoption system

It's May oan Arran
an' yon muckle African gowk
hunkers oan the sag
o' telephone wire
cooin' an' lookin'
aw vauntie.

Wit maks theym think
they can come o'er here,
howk oor wee wrens,
reed warblers, oor dunnocks
oot thur coorie-doons,
hurl thur egg-bairns
tae smatter oan the grund?

Wit maks theym sae lairdly
that thur sakeless parents
– a tenth the size o' theym –
fly o'er fifty mile a day
tae feed yon great geggie?

How come dae folks greet
tae *no'* hear thur crouse coos?

Parsonage

This house is a looking-glass,
the sisters only just
out of the reflection.
The stone floors grained with
sermons and laudanum, the tread
of Byronic heroes and moor-peat.
Their souls laying down layers
of passion in miniscule script,
the insect-pens scrabbling
from their hive-brain.

This home is a well-worn book,
covers creased with handgrime,
soot, dog-hair, corners
turned down lovingly. That familiar
creak on the stair, turn
of the clock's key, slide
of the sash to shut out
the owl-talk, the choke
of coal smoke, and that call
from the moor.

Brontë soundscape

This is the funeral bell
This is the turning of pages
This is the yowl of Gasper
This his skittering claws
on the pantry floor
This is the measuring tick
of the staircase clock
This the retching of Branwell
This is the scratching of pens
This is Tabby scouring the pots
And this is Emily's breath
on the rippled windowglass
mouthing *Heathcliff*
over and over.

Son of the Mother-whose-children-are-like-fish

for David Oluwale

At 19, the mouth of the Ogun breathes him out,
the Humber inhales him, but it's the Aire
that slithers through his sharp-dressed dances;
his college rejection; his Labour Exchange queue;
that (once Tetley'd) slakes his foundry heat.

Ellerker and Kitching are going white
stomping him through Allport's five stages.
The Loiner rain finds him wandering abroad
in 'the jungle' of Middy Woods, shop doorways,
Armley nick, Millgarth nick, the Dark Arches.

It's Mire Beck that circles his High Royds'
corridor-slur where friends hold him, and the nurse
chaperones his hand, dipping it to the water-blue
airmail: *Owon baba… Owon Yemoja…*

And then it's Stage 5 and the long-stanked Aire
holds him under.

But PC Galvin blows his whistle; Philips writes
'Lame Darkie'; Sandford's 'Smiling David' speaks
from British wirelesses; and when the 30-year-gag
coughs out police charge sheets marked 'Wog', it releases
a rush of art and outrage that keeps David alive.

Here he is, age 86. And in his garden
we hold him, hear his quick laugh.

This Tuesday morning she is travelling to the farthest arm of the galaxy

She spent all yesterday in training:
the exercises against gravity;
the moving safely around her cabin;
the gathering of supplies;
the careful donning
of her spacewalk suit.

At 10.12 GMT she gets the nod from Houston,
releases the airlock and immediately
the manoeuvre down the one small step
almost stalls the whole mission, but,

the last moment giant leap by the girl
with the worried dog, has the spacemobile
safely back on track and the pilot is in full
control as she eases her craft round the back

of the sheltered flats and into the wind-tunnel
by the park where her navigations systems
are pummelled by solar winds and passing
lorries. Finally, after a long communication

blackout with base, she reports in
from the safe-docking-refuge of the bench
that says: *This was Alan's favourite view*
before the ring road was built.

Half-a-light-year of R&R on the bench planet
and a re-fuelling of tea from her flask
and the pilot is gliding out into the galactic
airways, the twin moons of *Saturn*

– *your local electrical wholesalers* gleam
off her titanium hull. Her oxygen is running low
but the red glow of the Post Office heaves
into view just beyond the next constellation.

Unsung

We copy you down; Moon has its first guest.
A stark beauty all of its own; stand by.
Roger that. Then three hours they lay to rest.

A bunch of guys about to turn blue are blessed.
It's beautiful the power of that black sky.
You've heard of Mike? Well, he did all the rest.

Roger that. Then three hours they tried to rest
in Eagle's cramp while the Apollo guy
you've never heard of – Mike – did all the rest.

Buzz and Neil dozed while round them reeled a fest
of stars and that blue orb of home flew by.
Roger that. Then three hours they lay to rest.

Meantime Houston bleeped and Mike ran more tests.
One small step, some bagged dirt, one flag held high.
You ever heard of Mike? He did all the rest.

He ran more tests, fixed tea for them and sighed.
The lift-off blast knocked planted flag awry:
Roger that. Then three hours they tried to rest
while Houston bleeped and Mike did all the rest.

Christmas list carnage

Early each November she sends printed sheets;
a quick covering note: *Any changes, Ma?*
before her printer churns out any labels.
And so, I take up my black pen, and cull my friends.

Two years ago, eighteen paid the ferryman.
Last year, twenty-three assumed room temperature.
This year, it's reached its peak – a cacophony
of popping clogs: thirty-two gone.

From two-hundred-and-nine, my pals have been
scythed to a mere seven. We phone each other now –
every month; dread the letter from some unknown offspring
that another of us has gone Tango Uniform.

Going up

Here I am again,
with all the essentials:
Cox's apples, balm tissues,
a full report on your carrots,
The Racing Times, a big big smile,
and your clean pyjamas – full
of this morning's moor wind.
I shall tell you how I watched them
dancing in the garden,
like you will again
– one day very soon.

This is always
the anxious time:
how will you look;
will there be good news
or bad; will we be able
to talk – to really talk
(over the drip, the bleeping machines,
the white white sheets);
will I be able to make you laugh,
or will we have to mind your stitches;
will the grey formica of the overbed table
be strong enough for me
(hampered, only slightly,
by my support stockings)
to really give it laldy
showing you my latest
Flamenco moves?

Today I press the button
for the open sky.
You will be lounging on a cloud,
not in that stuffy ward.
I will feed you peeled red grapes
as the nurses float by with trolleys
of Turkish Delight, chilled G&Ts,
and those huge Toblerone you adore,
and I only ever thought to buy you
at Christmas.

Still

Listen.
There is a silence now.
This stillness.
Gradually we will get used to it.
But, for now,
it is strange.
You have left such a gap.

But listen closer.
All your laughter, all your love
is still ringing out.
Still holding us.

All our memories of you
are still with us.
All the love we shared
is still in every one of us.

And although we ache
from the loss of you,
you will always be here
as still and steady
as any star.

Acknowledgements

They just use dogs to get more dosh – it shouldn't be allowed
(Published in *Homeless* anthology Stairwell Books; *Songs for the Unsung* anthology Grey Hen Press; *The Big Issue*)

The inter-species dialogue of Columba palumbus
(Published in *The Valley Press Anthology of Yorkshire Poetry*)

Kestrel versus crow and Nest
(Published in *Zoomorphic* magazine)

Ardnamurchan dragonfly
(Published in *The Ver Prize* anthology)

Bee-dance
(Pubished in *The Garden* anthology Otley Word Feast Press)

Salmo salar
(Published in *Extraordinary Forms* anthology Grey Hen Press)

Coppice
(Published in Envoi Issue 157)

Necessary equipment for River Pigs
(Published by *The Interpreter's House*)

The straight lines of sea areas
(Published in *Running Before The Wind* anthology Grey Hen Press)

Horses always look cleverer than they are
(Highly commended in Torbay Open Poetry Comp. 2017)

Jam
(Published in *Butcher's Dog* magazine)

We are The Psoriasis Warriors
(Published in *Manchester Psoriasis Poetry Shout Out* chapbook)

The finding of parts
(Published in *The Bigger Picture* anthology S@veAs Writing Group Publishing)

The finding of parts and Lest we forget?
(Published in *Agenda – Requiem: The Great War*)

Lest we forget?
(Published in *The British Lichen Society Bulletin*)

This is where my hands used to be
(Published in *Prole* magazine)

This is the talking of hands
(Published in *Verse Matters* anthology Valley Press)

High Fidelity and Connection
(Second prize in 2016 Torbay Poetry Prize)

The F word
(Published in *My Dear Watson* anthology Beautiful Dragons Press)

The monitoring of punches
(Published in *The Ver Prize* anthology)

Herd
(Published in Acumen 81)

Mid-Atlantic ridge
(Published in *Slow Things* anthology Emma Press)

Desk-light
(Published on *York-Mix* website)

Love potion flask
(Published in *Spokes* anthology OWF Press)

The 'conservation nightmare' of the Ballachulish Goddess
(Published in *Verse Matters* anthology Valley Press)

Immigrants abuse Scottish adoption system
(Published in *Lallans* magazine)

Pogrom – Clifford's Tower, York
(Published in *Algebra Of Owls* e-zine)

Parsonage and Brontë soundscape
(Published in *The Scratching of Pens* anthology Like This Press and in *A Source Of Strange Delight* anthology Grey Hen Press)

Son of the Mother-whose-children-are-like-fish
(Joint first prize winner in 'Remembering Oluwale' poetry prize, and published in *Remembering Oluwale* anthology Valley Press; in *Songs for the Unsung* anthology Grey Hen Press; and in *Any change? Poetry in a Hostile Environment* anthology, ed. Ian Duhig)